T0247855

Almost

an

Elegy

Almost an
Elegy

New and Later Selected Poems

LINDA PASTAN

W. W. NORTON & COMPANY
Independent Publishers Since 1923

For information about permission to reproduce selections from this book, write to
Permissions, W. W. Norton & Company, Inc., 500 Fifth Avenue, New York, NY 10110

For information about special discounts for bulk purchases, please contact
W. W. Norton Special Sales at specialsales@wwnorton.com or 800-233-4830

Manufacturing by LSC Harrisonburg
Book design by Beth Steidle
Production manager: Louise Mattarelliano

Library of Congress Cataloging-in-Publication Data
Names: Pastan, Linda, 1932– author.
Title: Almost an elegy : new and later selected poems / Linda Pastan.
Description: First edition. | New York, NY: W. W. Norton & Company, [2022]
Identifiers: LCCN 2022027222 | ISBN 9781324021490 (cloth) |
ISBN 9781324021506 (epub)
Subjects: LCGFT: Poetry.
Classification: LCC PS3566.A775 A78 2022 | DDC 811/.54—dc23/eng/20220613
LC record available at https://lccn.loc.gov/2022027222

W. W. Norton & Company, Inc., 500 Fifth Avenue, New York, N.Y. 10110
www.wwnorton.com

W. W. Norton & Company Ltd., 15 Carlisle Street, London W1D 3BS

1 2 3 4 5 6 7 8 9 0

For Josephine

Acknowledgments

I would like to thank the following periodicals in which many of the poems in "New Poems" first appeared:

Beltway Poetry Quarterly; *Catamaran*; *Fledgling Rag*; *The Gettysburg Review*; *Jewish Journal*; *Moment*; *New Letters*; *The Paris Review*; *Plume*; *Poet Lore*; *Salmagundi*; *South Florida Poetry Journal*; *Southern Poetry Review*; *The Southampton Review*; *Virginia Quarterly Review*; and *Women's Review of Books*.

A stanza of "Summer Triptych" was featured in Poem-A-Day, by the Academy of American Poets.

Contents

New Poems

———

From *Queen of a Rainy Country* (2006)

From *Traveling Light* (2011)

From *Insomnia* (2015)

———

From *A Dog Runs Through It* (2018)

———

Almost

an

Elegy

New

Poems

MEMORY OF A BIRD

Paul Klee, watercolor and pencil on paper

What is left is a beak,
a wing,
a sense of feathers,

the rest lost
in a pointillist blur of tiny
rectangles.

The bird has flown,
leaving behind
an absence.

This is the very
essence
of flight—a bird

so swift
that only memory
can capture it.

ON THE SILL OF THE WORLD

On one wing, a quarter moon has moved across
the dark sky into morning,

and as I watch, a thousand leaves fly by,
loosed from their autumn trees.

So many wings: moths in their somber garments,
houseflies, the sound and shadow of a jet.

A tide of geese honks its long way south,
and one small girl attaching angel wings

to her nightgown
flits around the house.

Now a new generation of birds
is landing on the sill. I name them

as Adam did: Kingfisher . . . Crow . . .
for they are the same birds

immortal in their feathers
and primed for flight.

STING

A bee stung the palm
of your right hand,
or did you touch a nettle?

There was a swelling,
the burn of pain—
a poisoned flower blooming

in the flesh—
and neither ice
nor baking soda helped.

You carried it around—
right hand in left,
as if it belonged to somebody else,

and you were angry—
not at the possible bee whose buzz
was all you knew of it,

not at the nettle, hidden scourge
of the summer garden.
It was the wound itself that angered you,

an early soldier in the army of afflictions
waiting for us, even
in the innocent grass.

FOR MIRIAM, WHO HEARS VOICES

If the voices are there
you can't ignore them,
whether they come up through the floorboards
on a conduit of music
or in a rattle of words that make sounds
but no sense.

They can be messages from the sky
in the form of rain at the window, or in the cold
silent statements of snow.
Sometimes it's the dead talking,
and there is comfort in that

like listening to your parents in the next room,
and perhaps it's the same parents still talking
years after they've gone.

If you're lucky, the vowels
you hear are shaped like sleep—
simple cries from the thicket
of your dreams. You lie in bed.
If the voices are there, you listen.

A DIFFERENT KIND OF APRIL: FOR JOAN

This morning winter died—
its stinging winds blown out,

its snowflakes melted
even before they formed,

like children already named
but never conceived;

and summer began with thunder
bullying.

Heat like a hand presses down
on the heart.

No spring at all this year,
only a memory of green emerging,

of crocuses and forsythia. Of you
alive, walking

with me, mocking
my moody complaints about the weather.

I HOLD MY BREATH

1.

I keep calling up Weather to ask
if it's going to rain, though I'm standing
at the window and can see
the staccato drops already falling.
We were to meet only if the day was fine.
And so I call again, hoping that
whoever's in charge of the weather
can be made to change their plan.

2.

I hold my breath at every stop light,
and if I don't breathe before it changes
I'll have good luck all day.

3.

I think of a child kneeling beside his bed,
blessing his mother, his father;
then blessing the bicycle, the dog,
the sailboat he solemnly asks for.

4.

At nine my father was told by the rabbi
that if he kissed a crucifix, he'd die.
He made one out of the live branches
of a tenement tree, stripping the greening leaves,
and he kissed it, frightened but refusing
what he'd been told. He lived
to watch me take charge of the weather.

TRUCE

This is for my surgeon father at last
whom I've desecrated in poem after poem
for punishing me with silence, for caring too much
about the exact degree of love and respect
my adolescent self let trickle down to him.
Who in one of his many depressions painted
still life after still life (our apartment rank
with brushes and turpentine and rotting vegetables)
painting himself back to sanity.

My father knew "Evangeline" by heart
and studded his letters to me with scraps
of poetry, though he never took note of mine.
He made up bedtime stories that always ended with
" and then there was an explosion . . ." but
I didn't inherit his gift for plot. His patients
called him charismatic (his doctor jokes, the airplanes
he made out of tongue depressors for the children)
and my friends turned up at his funeral, saying
they'd always wanted a father like mine.

How well he hid the archeology of grief.
His extended family had disappeared in Poland,
though he never spoke of them, and he never
stopped grieving for my stillborn brother. He badly
wanted a son, and I was just a girl.

Is there somewhere in the afterlife where he can read
what I write about him? Maybe he'd acknowledge at last
how alike we were in holding grudges;
in loving and caring too much; in somehow
painting ourselves, with brush or pen,
back to the kind of fragile truce we could live with.

KRISTALLNACHT

was the word I heard
my parents whisper behind
closed doors. And I pictured
the world under a sudden
enchantment of ice, each tree limb
braceleted in crystal, each lamppost,
each windshield glazed
and electrically gleaming,
the very air wincing with light.
And the only sound would be
a myriad tinkling,
as of a thousand thousand
miniature wind chimes.
The treacherous beauty of words!
Crystal night: the stars themselves
blazing and frozen in place.

INSTRUCTION

You must rock your pain in your arms
until it's asleep, then leave it

in a darkened room
and tiptoe out.

For a moment you will feel
the emptiness of peace.

But in the next room
your pain is already stirring.

Soon it will be
calling your name.

ALMOST AN ELEGY: FOR TONY HOAGLAND

Your poems make me want
to write my poems,

which is a kind of plagiarism
of the spirit.

But when your death reminds me
that mine is on its way,

I close the book, clinging
to this tenuous world the way the leaves

outside cling to their tree
just before they turn color and fall.

I need time to read all the poems
you left behind, which pierce

the darkness here at my window
but did nothing to save you.

CLASS NOTES

My high school class of 1950
is disappearing over the edge
of the world—a snowless avalanche.
Rosalie of the pancake makeup;
Alex who outran us even towards death;
three Susans, two Davids, and a Roger.

When I see our class representative's
name on an incoming email,
I think of how families must have felt
during World War II when they saw
the Western Union bicycle approaching.

And I remember all of us lining up
in gym class as captains chose their teams.
The line would dwindle until, on one leg
then the other, I was standing almost alone.
Maybe whoever is doing the choosing now
thinks that I would be no good at dying.

THE TOURIST

We saw the entrance
to the underworld

outside of Naples,
just after eating pizza

at that special place
and before

boarding the ferry
to Capri.

We could tick it off
our list of sights to see,

but there was nothing
to see.

Ground bleached of features.
Colorless air.

And remembering Odysseus
and his journey here,

meeting the ghost
of his long dead mother,

we felt cheated,
as if someone

from our growing list
of lost friends

should have emerged
to greet us.

SQUINT,

and that low line
of blue cloud
hovering
over the treetops

could be an ocean—the roar
of the highway
the clamorous waves
breaking.

And that dark shape menacing
your every footstep
could be no more
than your own obedient shadow.

See whatever you want
to see. Even
at the moment of death
forget the door

opening on darkness.
See instead
the familiar faces
you thought were lost.

TULIPS IN A GLASS VASE

their huge, tear-shaped
petals fall
all over the rug

these tulips
in the last throes
of life

weeping
their colors—flame,
purple, creamy white—

while outside
spring
in all its ornamental

mania
blossoms on
and on without them

PLUNDER: TO A YOUNG FRIEND

On a day of windy transition, one season to the next,
you spoke of helping your mother close her house,
of the choices you had to make—what to discard,
what to keep—as if it were your childhood itself
waiting to be plundered. You kept a Persian rug,
all reds and golds, to walk on every day,
keeping the past alive under your feet;
those nested Russian dolls you played with
as a girl: grandmother, mother, daughter;
four bentwood chairs wrenched from their table.

I listened, thinking I'd be next to try
to crowd a lifetime of things
into a shrinking universe of boxes.
I've started dismantling my life already, throwing
out letters from people I remember loving,
choosing among books—this one to stay,
that one to go—as if I were a judge
sentencing some to death, the rest
to the purgatory of the emptying shelf.
Perhaps I should simply burn it all.

But don't we live on in what we've left behind?
In the fading twilight of Kodak? In our sterling
knives and spoons tarnishing on a grandchild's
casual table? Don't these become
a kind of museum of the afterlife?
The Pharaohs had it right. They took
their whole world with them—vases and chests,
gilded statues, jewels—plundered perhaps,
but not for a thousand years.
Nefertiti's tomb has never been found.

ODE TO MY CAR KEY

Silver bullet
shape of a treble clef
I slip you
in the ignition—
an arrow
seeking its target—
where you fit
like a thread
in the eye
of a needle
like a man and
a woman.
A click and
the engine roars,
the road unscrolls
on its way
to anywhere.
At night you sleep
in the darkness
of a drawer,
on a pillow
of tarnished coins.
Oh faithful key:
last week I gave
you up
for good—
Excalibur back
in its stone—
as I climbed into
the waiting vehicle
of old age.

CATARACTS

Like frosted glass,
you blur the hard edges
of the cruel world.

Like summer fog, you obscure
the worst even an ocean can do.
But watch out.

They are coming for you
with their sterile instruments,
their sharpened knives,

saying I will be made new—
as if I were a rich man
wanting a younger wife.

Soon the world will be all glare.
Grass will turn a lethal green,
flower petals a chaos

of blood reds, shocking pink.
What will I see? I am afraid
of so much clarity, so much light.

APARTMENT LIFE

Is this what a hive is,
each bee in its own cell,
that constant hum,
the queen a kind of manager
collecting the rent?
Footsteps overhead, people dancing,
or fighting, or making love on the floor
(then sheepish smiles
in the elevator—not friendly exactly,
but more than polite, like dogs sniffing
each other before deciding
whether to play or growl).
The ghosts of cooking
haunt the walls.
Hallways are labyrinths
in a nightmare,
but they lead us home, door
double locked, the clicks of safety
like clicks of the tongue
on the roof of an anxious mouth.
Turtles all the way down,
each in its own shell.
I think of all the compartments
I've known: eggs in their cardboard cartons,
chocolates in frilly paper squares,
boxes within boxes, above
and below, on either side.
So many other lives lived
mysteriously, giving out only hints—
shreds of overheard music
seeping under the door.

THE CLOUDS

From a high window
I watch the clouds—

armada
of white sails

blown by the wind
from west to east, as if

auditioning for me,
as if they needed

nothing more
than to be in a poem.

THE QUARRY, PONTOISE

Pissarro, 1875

To enter into the greens
of this picture—
forest, emerald, jade—
is to drown in the bristle of
pine needles or in leaves
that are more than leaves
the way landscapes in dreams
are more than themselves,
dredged as they are
in the colors of sleep.
On the long road winding its way
through the painting,
I can just make out
a small woman, dwarfed
in this universe of color
but alive still
in the green, intractable
mysteries of paint.

INTERIOR, WOMAN AT THE WINDOW

Caillebotte, 1880

From the fringes of Impressionism,
Caillebotte gave us this serious interior,
this woman with the serene back
gazing out into morning
while the man with the mustache,
dressed in the same shades of muted color,
gazes at a newspaper on his lap.

The device I rented to hear an expert on Art
is murmuring in my ear:
that this painting, for instance, is a study
in Psychological Isolation. And yet
what it reminds me of is breakfast
this morning, looking out the window
at the sun just grazing the treetops

while my husband enfolds himself
in not just one but in two newspapers.
Intimacy, I'd call this, not isolation—
the trick of being apart
and together at the same time,
as each of us lets something of the world
into the coffee-scented kitchen.

ANONYMOUS

"Summer is y-comen in . . ."
you wrote,
and "Lady
queen of Paradise . . ."
And from a phone booth
you called police
to tell them what you saw.

Man or woman, hiding
in plain sight—that shadow
behind us in the mirror—
you pledge your dollars
on the radio, mail
grueling information
in an unmarked envelope.

You aren't modest:
being invisible is your power,
and it survives the ages.
Nameless . . . incognito . . . lost
in a crowd. Under the neutral sky
we all die anonymous.
"Loude sing cuckoo."

REREADING *ANNA KARENINA* FOR THE
FIFTH TIME

I'm still looking
for the translation where
she says no to Vronsky;

where despite Chekhov,
a dangerous train at the beginning
doesn't have to mean death by train

at the end. Meanwhile I can
concentrate on Levin and Kitty,
on that happy domesticity

we all surely wish for.
In Russia, the temperatures of passion
and weather are both extreme.

I must wrap
my delicate hands in a muff
to keep out the cold.

I must let my desires
burn safely,
not between the covers

of a carved, four-poster bed,
but between the worn covers
of this book.

CRIMES

"Si trattava di sentire le cose e disporle nell' unico posto ad esse riservato. Come scrivere versi, appunto."
MARCELLO FOIS, *SEMPRE CARO*

When the Italian poet/detective
tells us that writing a poem
is the same as solving a crime,
I know what he means.

Each line is a piece of a jigsaw
waiting to fit in a stanza: the scarlet
curve of a witness's smile or an edge
of blue lake where the body was found.

And every iamb
is searching for justice.
"The right words find themselves
without knowing how," we're told.

The narrators all are unreliable—
criminals inventing
their perfect alibis, poets
lying in order to tell the truth.

And each partial metaphor,
like a good investigator, searches
for its other half— the clue
that explains everything.

Solving a crime,
you may argue, is often
a matter of life or death.
Exactly, I answer.

HOW FAR WOULD YOU TRUST YOUR ART?

Stephen Dunn, "If a Clown"

As far as light travels
from the star that's wished on
to the wish itself.

As far as I could throw
a book of poems
underhand.

As far as syllables move
from my mouth
to your retreating ear

and as far as the journey love makes
all the way to indifference
then back to love.

As far as the bee slaloms
through the flowers,
laden with honey.

As far as the eye
can see
blindfolded.

As far as the trail of ink
meanders
over the virgin page.

Or as the poet said
of swimming to save his daughter,
as far as is needed.

MIRAGE

I have been writing about death since
I was not much more than a child,
constructing it from all the books I read
under the covers, after lights out—
Beth in *Little Women*, for instance,
or the parents in *The Secret Garden*.
I loved the melodrama of it, the stoic tears.
Though I was jolted when my Aunt Hilda

tried to jump into her husband's grave
and had to be restrained by clucking friends
and relatives, while I looked on,
sandwiched between my parents,
in the back row of my first cemetery.
It's much simpler now that I can approximate
the number of years before death overtakes,
then takes me. Ninety approaches.
And instead of drama, or even fear,

I want to simply be one with the trees sighing
outside my window, sighing not for me
but to accommodate the wind.
I want to devour the sky just after sunset when
color leached from the sun spreads
like a flaming mirage over what clouds there are.
At night instead of sheep
I catalog my children and grandchildren,

how each is faring. Some of them act as though
the whole wide world is holding its breath, waiting
just for them. And I appreciate such innocence.
Looking back on the scenery of my own life—the maple desk
where I sat, trying to make stories of death my own—
I try to remember exactly when innocence turned
into something else. To the kind of knowledge
I live with now. To what feels almost like longing.

THE COLLECTED POEMS

They take you through my life
one poem at a time,
memory's beast raging
through the pages

inventing as it goes—
the slap that was really
a caress, the tears no more
than a mirage.

My actual childhood
was a sapling
in the forest of years,
yet it shadows these poems

so that my mother's death,
for instance, sheds its leaves
over everything.
So many leaves.

For years I wrestled
with syllables, with silence.
My stories were love
and its hazardous weather;

feathers of snow, of birds
ghosting the windows;
sharpened needles waiting
in every innocent haystack.

Now I rest
in a hammock of words, waiting
for the sun to rise again
over the horizon of the page.

SUMMER TRIPTYCH

1.

The world is water
to these bronzed boys
on their surfboards,
riding the waves
of Maui
like so many fearless
cowboys, challenging
death on bucking
broncos of foam.

2.

On the beach at Santorini
we ate those tiny silver fish
grilled straight from the sea,
and when the sun went down
in the flaming west
there was applause
from all the sated diners,
as if it had done its acrobatic plunge
just for them.

3.

Swathed from head to toe
in seeming veils of muslin,
the figure in the Nantucket fog
poles along the shoreline on a flat barge.
It could be Charon
transporting souls. Or just
another fisherman in a hoodie,
trolling for bluefish
on the outgoing tide.

LIGHTNING

Neon zigzag . . .
migraine embedded in cloud . . .
I draw all the blinds,
hide in the darkened basement.
The rumble of thunder
like a feared uncle threatening
from the next room.
Even the dog trembles,
the fur on a cartoon cat stands on end,
its paw caught in a live socket.
Fluorescence blinding
every window.
There was a meeting
of people struck by lightning
who lived to proudly tell of it,
and Captain Marvel
wears its emblem
bright on his chest. Think
of Ben Franklin's crazy kite probing
for answers. Still,
the barometer tumbles,
a sizzle of fear splits the night sky.
It's Zeus, high on amphetamines, aiming
his bolts in my direction.

AT THE WINERY

1.

The grapes are as round,
as smooth as beads
a child might string together
and wear like pearls
around her neck.

2.

Asleep for years
in the barrel: a dark purple sea
with no tide, only the slow
invisible change from prose
to poetry.

3.

Syrah ... Pinot Noir ...
Chardonnay ...
Voluptuous sound of a cork
surrendering.

4.

The answer
to every question:
Intoxication.

5.

The vintner is old now,
shriveled and small.
In the lush air, sour-sweet
hint of raisins.

AUTUMN: FOR JANE KENYON

Let autumn come
with its acorns and leaf smoke,
its bronze bells tolling.

Let the school doors open
and the children, like small penitents, march
into their classrooms.

Let the subway grates become bed frames
preparing themselves for the homeless.
Let autumn come.

And the trees will succumb
to rust, to brown,
the trees will go naked.

And the grass will fade,
green will be almost
forgotten.

Shake out your coats
from the blizzard
of moth balls.

Sharpen your pencils, their shavings
the color of leaf fall.
Let autumn come.

AWAY

In the small craft
that is my body, I am
ready to take off

from the shore,
waving goodbye
to the faces

I've loved,
not sad exactly
but anxious

to catch
the outgoing
tide.

THE FUTURE

When do we trade the future for the past?
A farmer plows his fields one final time.
I think each poem I write will be the last.

The world grows small; it used to seem so vast.
Retirees lie in bed 'til after nine
(when do we trade the future for the past?)

they pull on trousers, sigh and cut the grass.
And I have lost the lust for making rhyme,
I think each poem I write will be the last.

The words come slowly now; they once came fast.
Each fledgling ode becomes a hill to climb.
When do we trade the future for the past?

There's TV and the crossword—days will pass,
walks on hard pavement—cities etched in grime.
I fear each poem I write will be the last.

Uncoupled, metaphors go streaming past.
The young are on their way, I watch them shine.
When did I trade the future for the past?
I think this poem I'm writing is the last.

From
The Last Uncle

2002

WOMEN ON THE SHORE

The pills I take to postpone death
are killing me, and the healing
journey we pack for waits
with its broken airplane,
the malarial hum of mosquitos.
Even the newly mowed domestic grass
hides fault lines in the earth
which could open at any time

and swallow us.
In Edvard Munch's woodcut,
the pure geometry of color—an arctic sky,
the luminescent blues and greens of water—
surrounds the woman in black
whose head is turning to a skull.
If death is everywhere we look,
at least let's marry it to beauty.

PRACTICING

My son is practicing the piano.
He is a man now, not the boy
whose lessons I once sat through,
whose reluctant practicing
I demanded—part of the obligation
I felt to the growth
and composition of a child.

Upstairs my grandchildren are sleeping,
though they complained earlier of the music
which rises like smoke up through the floorboards,
coloring the fabric of their dreams.
On the porch my husband watches the garden fade
into summer twilight, flower by flower;
it must be a little like listening to the fading

diminuendo notes of Mozart.
But here where the dining-room table
has been pushed aside to make room
for this second- or third-hand upright,
my son is playing the kind of music
it took him all these years,
and sons of his own, to want to make.

TEARS

"Save us from tears that bring no healing..."
MATTHEW ARNOLD

When the ophthalmologist told me gravely
that I didn't produce enough tears,
I wanted to say: but I cry too much
and too often. At airports and weddings
and sunsets. At movies

where the swell of sentimental music
forces open my tear ducts
like so many locks in a canal.
And when he handed me this vial
of artificial tears, I wanted to tell him

about Niobe. Perhaps if her tear ducts
had been deficient, she wouldn't
have dissolved into salty water
after the loss of her children.
Maybe other heroes and heroines

deprived of the resonant ability to cry
would have picked themselves up
and acted sensibly. Othello for instance
who wept, before he killed her,
into Desdemona's embroidered pillow.

And so I take this bottle of distilled grief
and put it in the back of a drawer,
but I don't throw it away. There may be poems
in the future that need to be watered,
for I still remember Tennyson

who wrote of how short swallow-flights of song
dip their wings in tears, and skim away.

GRACE

When the young professor folded
his hands at dinner and spoke to God
about my safe arrival
through the snow, thanking Him also
for the food we were about to eat,

it was in the tone of voice I use
to speak to friends when I call
and get their answering machines,
chatting about this and that
in a casual voice,

picturing them listening
but too busy to pick up the phone
or out taking care of important
business somewhere else.
The next day, flying home

through a windy
and overwhelming sky, I knew
I envied his rapport with God
and hoped his prayers
would keep my plane aloft.

THE COSSACKS: FOR F

For Jews, the Cossacks are always coming.
Therefore I think the sun spot on my arm
is melanoma. Therefore I celebrate
New Year's Eve by counting
my annual dead.

My mother, when she was dying,
spoke to her visitors of books
and travel, displaying serenity
as a form of manners, though
I could tell the difference.

But when I watched you planning
for a life you knew
you'd never have, I couldn't explain
your genuine smile in the face
of disaster. Was it denial

laced with acceptance? Or was it
generations of being English—
Brontë's Lucy in *Villette*
living as if no fire raged
beneath her dun-colored dress.

I want to live the way you did,
preparing for next year's famine with wine
and music as if it were a ten-course banquet.
But listen: those are hoofbeats
on the frosty autumn air.

POTSY

The cards that come each Christmas
bear signatures from another life.
I line them on the mantel in the kind of rows
we stood in for school pictures,
and the names are the same:
Lila so fleet of foot, the bobbles
on her socks like the wings
of Mercury as she ran; Rowena
playing potsy; Gerda with her braids
and budding irony—girls
I've lost, except at Christmastime,
whose voices once bloomed daily
on the phone (their numbers fixed
like music in my mind: Tremont 2
and Endicott 9). Sometimes I think
we keep in touch each year
so we will recognize each other
in the life to come, when we leave
our womanly disguises behind
and circle back to the past,
the way we did playing potsy
when we jumped from square
to square, ending
on square one where we began,
with daylight fading, though
we hardly noticed it, ignoring
our mothers who were calling us
to supper and our separate lives.

BESS

When Bess, the landlord's black-eyed
daughter, waited for her highwayman
in the poem I learned by breathless
heart at twelve, it occurred to me

for the first time that my mild-eyed
mother Bess might have a life
all her own—a secret past
I couldn't enter, except in dreams.

That single sigh of a syllable
has passed like a keepsake
to this newest child, wrapped now
in the silence of sleep.

And in the dream I enter,
I could be holding my infant mother
in my arms: the same wide cheekbones,
the name indelible as a birthmark.

ARMONK

In sleep I summon it—dark green shutters
opening on my childhood, white clapboards
bathed in the purple shadows
of azaleas, the perfect 18th-century
farmhouse—"Armonk" we called it,
as if there were no village of that name.
How we loved the old, contorted apple trees
of Armonk, the revolutionary musket
in all its ornamental firepower hanging
over our mantel, the plain pine furniture
assembled from a more strictly crafted age.
It was as though we longed to be part
of a history that could replace our own
ancestors' broken nights in the shtetl
with the softly breaking light
of an American morning.

But what is history if not the imagination
of descendants, made almost flesh?
In old photographs, the cook holds high
a platter of Thanksgiving turkey,
an aunt waves from a mullioned window,
my mother, at her needle and thread, smiles
her understated smile. This
is my authentic childhood.
And my orthodox grandfather, hunched
over a table, dealing out cards
in an endless game of pinochle,
straightens up for the camera.
Patriarch of the armchair, he could be
some early New England governor
posing for posterity in his starched
white shirt and dark cravat.

THE LAST UNCLE

The last uncle is pushing off
in his funeral skiff (the usual
black limo) having locked
the doors behind him
on a whole generation.

And look, we are the elders now
with our torn scraps
of history, alone
on the mapless shore
of this raw new century.

HUSBANDRY

You move the sprinkler
from green to deeper green,
from threads of grass to
pin cushions of moss,

walking among your young plants
like the Creator himself
inventing rain,
or like the recluse artist

Ni Zan who left his cave
to wash the paulownia trees
by hand, as if they were
his children.

GHIACCIO

At Herculaneum, where
steaming lava once crept
like a live and panting animal
over alleys and doorsteps, I fell
and broke my ankle. And lying
on the dusty ground, a tourist attraction
for passersby myself,
I wondered how, hobbled,
I would escape from lava or ash
or other more pedestrian dangers.
There is nothing like the sound
of bone cracking
to shift the axis of the earth,
and pain is never impersonal
but calls us by our given names.
In that ancient place, where the very sea
once fled its boundaries,
where antique human bones were found
heaped together—so many pieces
in an intricate puzzle now
but vulnerable once, and ordinary as mine,
I watched my ankle swell
to an unfamiliar, foreign shape;
and helpless, I tried to think
of the Italian word for ice.

THE DEATH OF THE BEE

> "The death of wild bee populations has become widespread..."
> NEWS REPORT

The biography of the bee
is written in honey
and is drawing
to a close.

Soon the buzzing
plainchant of summer
will be silenced
for good;

the flowers, unkindled,
will blaze
one last time
and go out.

And the boy nursing
his stung ankle this morning
will look back
at his brief tears

with something
like regret,
remembering the amber
taste of honey.

From

Queen of a Rainy

Country

2006

A TOURIST AT ELLIS ISLAND

I found him, Jankel Olenik,
age 3, on the manifest
of the ship *Spaarndam*
in 1902—my surgeon father
Jack, of the silk ties
and trimmed mustache,
who never mentioned
the life he once inhabited
not just in a different language

but in a different book,
its pages yellowed at the edges.
He thrust me into the new world
scrubbed clean of peasant dirt,
whole chapters of my history
torn out. Failed
archeologist of memory,
I never asked
a single question.

MAIDEN NAME

My daughter's teacher is named
Olenik—my maiden name,
and Olenik was the name of a therapist
I talked to once about my dread of lightning—
I finally bought a lightning rod instead.
There's even a Russian poet who spells
his name with a c instead of a k
but may share my taste
for melancholy, my ice-blue Slavic eyes.
Are we defined by names, or
was Adam merely arbitrary, pointing
at some wooly creature and legislating: lamb?
I was never really a maiden anyway,
not the way I like to think of that word—
Rapunzel or the milkmaids in Elizabethan lyrics,
and I haven't used Olenik in fifty years.
But hearing that name spill out again so casually
from my daughter's shapely Olenik mouth
is like waking up after a too-long sleep
and having to rub the syllables from my eyes.

PARTING THE WATERS

Nothing is lost.
The past surfaces
from the salted tide pool
of oblivion over
and over again,
and here it is now—
complete
with ironed sheets, old sins,
and pewter candlesticks.
My mother and aunts approach,
shaking the water from
their freshly washed hair
like aging mermaids.
They have been here
all along, sewing
or reading a book, waiting
for the wand of memory
to touch them.

I MARRIED YOU

I married you
for all the wrong reasons,
charmed by your
dangerous family history,
by the innocent muscles, bulging
like hidden weapons
under your shirt,
by your naive ties, the colors
of painted scraps of sunset.

I was charmed too
by your assumptions
about me: my serenity—
that mirror waiting to be cracked,
my flashy acrobatics with knives
in the kitchen.
How wrong we both were
about each other,
and how happy we have been.

50 YEARS

Though we know
how it will end:
in grief and silence,
we go about our ordinary days
as if the acts of boiling an egg
or smoothing down a bed
were so small
they must be overlooked
by death. And perhaps

the few years left, sun-drenched
but without grand purpose,
will somehow endure,
the way a portrait of lovers endures
radiant and true on the wall
of some obscure Dutch museum,
long after the names
of the artist and models
have disappeared.

FIRING THE MUSE

I am giving up the muse Calliope.
I have told her to pack up her pens and her inks
and to take her lyrical smile,
her coaxing ways, back to Mt. Helicon,
or at least to New York.
I will even write her a reference if she likes
to someone whose head is still fizzy
with iambs and trochees,
someone still hungry for the scent of laurel,
the taste of fame, for the pure astonishment of seeing
her own words blaze up on the page.
Let me lie in this hammock in the fading sun
without guilt or longing, just a glass
of cold white wine in one hand,
not even a book in the other. A dog
will lie at my feet who can't read anyway,
loving me just for myself, and for
the biscuit I keep concealed in my pocket.

REREADING FROST

Sometimes I think all the best poems
have been written already,
and no one has time to read them,
so why try to write more?

At other times though,
I remember how one flower
in a meadow already full of flowers
somehow adds to the general fireworks effect

as you get to the top of a hill
in Colorado, say, in high summer
and just look down at all that brimming color.
I also try to convince myself

that the smallest note of the smallest
instrument in the band,
the triangle for instance,
is important to the conductor

who stands there, pointing his finger
in the direction of the percussions,
demanding that one silvery ping.
And I decide not to stop trying,

at least not for a while, though in truth
I'd rather just sit here reading
how someone else has been acquainted
with the night already, and perfectly.

HEAVEN

Are there seasons in heaven?
In God's anteroom are there windows
that look out on trees like these—

each leaf a note for the brass
ensemble of autumn—
the dry ones castanets

clicking: October, October.
Can heaven itself be golden
enough to rival all this?

GEOGRAPHY

I am haunted by the names
of foreign places: Lvov and its bells;
Galway with its shimmer of green;
Grudnow and Minsk
where my grandfather's famished face
belongs on the tarnished coins.

I am haunted by the weight of all those histories:
coronations and christenings; massacres,
famines—people shoveled
under the dark earth, just so much compost,
the lowly potato failing in Ireland,
like daylight itself failing at noon.

Oh, the vastness of maps,
the perfect roundness of globes—
those bellies pregnant with the names
of unimaginable townships and cities. Atlantis
and the Isles of the Blest are not as haunting to me
as Guangzhou or Xi'an or Santorini.

A for Ancona, an operator intones,
N for Napoli, T for Turino,
and at her voice longitudes and latitudes
become entangled like fishnets, waves
of people migrate across borders and oceans
and through the teeming streets of Buenos Aires.

While I remain quietly here in my anonymous woods
where the stream beyond the kitchen window
is so small it is only visible when it creams to ice,
where even in spring, resurgent with rain,
all it can do is empty itself into another stream,
also small, also nameless.

LEAVING THE ISLAND

We roll up rugs and strip the beds by rote,
summer expires as it has done before.
The ferry is no simple pleasure boat

nor are we simply cargo, though we'll float
alongside heavy trucks—their stink and roar.
We roll up rugs and strip the beds by rote.

This bit of land whose lines the glaciers wrote
becomes the muse of memory once more;
the ferry is no simple pleasure boat.

I'll trade my swimsuit for a woolen coat;
the torch of autumn has but small allure.
We roll up rugs and strip the beds by rote.

The absences these empty shells denote
suggest the losses winter has in store.
The ferry is no simple pleasure boat.

The songs of summer dwindle to one note:
the fog horn's blast (which drowns this closing door).
We rolled up rugs and stripped the beds by rote.
The ferry is no simple pleasure boat.

DEATH IS INTENDED

"On Feb. 6, 2000, 67-year-old Guy Waterman, naturalist, outdoorsman, devoted husband . . . decided to climb a New Hampshire mountain, lie down on the cold stones and die overnight of exposure. 'Death is intended,' he wrote."
THE NEW YORK TIMES BOOK REVIEW

" . . . the melancholy beauty of giving it all up."
ROBERT HASS

Isn't that what the Inuit did when they were old,
dragged themselves through a wilderness
of ice and up some mountain?
Then they could fall asleep forever,
their dark eyes speckled with falling snow—
not suicide exactly, but the opening
of a door so death could enter.
"Quit while you're ahead," my father told me
as I was feeding quarters into slot machines.
And that's what Waterman did, he quit
before infirmity could catch him, or other afflictions
whose breath he could already smell.
But I wanted more: a waterfall of coins
spilt on my lap, the raw, electric charge
of money. I came away with nothing;
but I still want more, if only more chapters
in the family book I'm part of: I want
to read all the unfolding stories, each child
a mystery only time can solve.
Was it bravery or cowardice what Waterman did,
or are those simply two sides of a coin,
like the coin some casual God might flip,
deciding who would live or die that day?
I'd rather flip the coin myself, but not at 67.
And not quite yet at 70, as spring
streams in over our suburban hills, enflaming
even the white New Hampshire mountains.

WHAT WE ARE CAPABLE OF

On reading of prisoner abuse at Abu Ghraib

What we are capable of
is always astonishing,
though never quite a surprise.

"Astronomers find more evidence
of dark matter," the newspaper says
on the next page—a fact or metaphor?

I think of those villagers in France
who risked their only lives
to save a handful of Jews, and I try

to find from that fading chink of light
an incandescent path
through all these darknesses.

WHY ARE YOUR POEMS SO DARK?

Isn't the moon dark too,
most of the time?

And doesn't the white page
seem unfinished

without the dark stain
of alphabets?

When God demanded light,
he didn't banish darkness.

Instead he invented
ebony and crows

and that small mole
on your left cheekbone.

Or did you mean to ask
"why are you sad so often?"

Ask the moon.
Ask what it has witnessed.

A RAINY COUNTRY

"Je suis comme le roi d'un pays pluvieux"
BAUDELAIRE

The headlines and feature stories alike
leak blood all over the breakfast table,
the wounding of the world mingling
with smells of bacon and bread.

Small pains are merely anterooms for larger,
and every shadow has a brother, just waiting.
Even grace is sullied by ancient angers.
I must remember it has always been like this:

those Trojan women, learning their fates;
the sharpness of the guillotine.
A filigree of cruelty adorns every culture.
I've thumbed through the pages of my life,

longing for childhood whose failures
were merely personal, for all
the stations of love I passed through.
Shadows and the shadow of shadows.

I am like the queen of a rainy country,
powerless and grown old. Another morning
with its quaint obligations: newspaper,
bacon grease, rattle of dishes and bones.

From
Traveling Light

2011

THE BURGLARY

They stole my mother's silver,
melting it down, perhaps,

into pure mineral, worth
only its own weight.

We must eat with our hands now,
grab for food

in this new place of greed,
our table set

only with memories, tarnishing
even as we speak:

my mother holding a shining ladle
in her hand,

serving the broth
to children who will forget

to polish her silver, forget even
to lock the house.

While forks and spoons are divided
from all purpose,

patterns are lost like friezes
after centuries of rain,

and every knife is robbed
of its cutting edge.

BREAD

after Lyubomir Levchev

"It seems to be the five stages
of yeast, not grief,
you like to write about,"
my son says,
meaning that bread
is always rising
and falling, being broken
and eaten, in my poems.
And though he is only half serious,
I want to say to him

"bread rising in the bowl
is like breath rising in the body";
or "if you knead the dough
with perfect tenderness,
it's like gently kneading flesh
when you make love."
Baguette . . . pita . . . pane . . .
challah . . . naan: bread is
the universal language, translatable
on the famished tongue.

Now it is time to open
the package of yeast
and moisten it with water,
watching for its fizz,
its blind energy—proofing
it's called, the animate proof
of life. Everything
is ready: salt, flour, oil.
Breadcrumbs are what lead
the children home.

MARCH

A cardinal is back in the tangled branches
of the maple. Edna always said "Red bird,
cold weather," but it's March now,
the buds already pinking on the camellias.
Edna used to roll biscuits before she cleaned our house,
singing "Amazing Grace" as she worked.
When I sent the tape of a poem to a magazine,
her song by chance on the flip side,
they rejected the poem but asked
if they could use "Amazing Grace."
She died last year, and now I think
her serenity was the flip side
of sadness—the grandson
in trouble with the law; the daughter
far away; so many rooms to clean.

My father's birthday punctuates March.
He would be a hundred and ten, and now
I'm three years older than he was when he died,
so many things unspoken between us.
This is the month for remembering, the light
so new it illuminates what we hardly knew we saw:
Edna in the room downstairs, alone;
my father wanting something from me
I didn't know to give.
It's such a mixed up month, one foot
in winter the other in spring, doing a windy
two-step from past to future;
while outside the cardinal on the leafless tree
performing its own Amazing Grace
is either scolding or serenading us.

LILACS

I am following lilacs
cluster by
purple cluster

from Whitman's
dooryards in April
north to New York

where my mother's garden
drowns in their scent
even without her.

I remember her gathering them
by the armful, blossoms
as plump and pale

as lavender pillows,
the white ones
paler still, shedding

their tiny florets
like baby teeth
over her polished floors.

Now in late May,
somewhere near Boston
they are still blooming,

their leaves as heart-shaped
as memory itself.
If I keep traveling north

I may finally find myself
somewhere beyond the treeline,
beyond loss.

For though I don't believe
in ghosts, I am haunted
by lilacs.

EVE ON HER DEATHBED

In the end we are no more than our own stories:
mine a few brief passages in the Book,
no further trace of plot or dialogue.
But I once had a lover no one noticed
as he slipped through the pages, through
the lists of those begotten and begetting.
Does he remember our faltering younger selves,
the pleasures we took while Adam,
a good bureaucrat, busied himself
with naming things, even after Eden?
What scraps will our children remember of us
to whom our story is simple
and they themselves the heroes of it?

I woke that first day with Adam for company,
and the tangled path I would soon follow
I've tried to forget: the animals, stunned
at first in the forest; the terrible, beating wings
of the angel; the livid curse of childbirth to come.
And then the children themselves,
loving at times, at times unmerciful.
Because of me there is just one narrative
for everyone, one indelible line from birth to death,
with pain or lust, with even love or murder
only brief diversions, subplots.

But what I think of now,
in the final bitterness of age,
is the way the garden groomed itself
in the succulent air of summer—each flower
the essence of its own color; the way even
the serpent knew it had a part it had to play, if
there were to be a story at all.

YEARS AFTER THE GARDEN

Years after the garden closed on Adam
a thousand thousand gardens take its place
(hold my hand, I hear the waters rising)
roses, lemons, lilac, hemlock, grape.

A thousand thousand gardens take its place.
Is each an Eden waiting to be lost?
Roses, lemons, lilac, hemlock, grape.
What was God thinking when he made the apple?

Is each an Eden waiting to be lost?
Seeds of knowledge, carelessness, and greed.
What was God thinking when he made the apple?
Did he do it only for the story?

Seeds of knowledge, carelessness, and greed—
they say the ice cap is already melting.
Did he do it only for the story?
Meringues of childhood melted on the tongue.

They say the ice cap is already melting.
The angel still waits with his flaming sword.
Meringues of childhood melted on the tongue,
but innocence alone will never save us.

The angel still waits with his flaming sword:
flowers and vegetables, forests tremble.
Innocence alone will never save us.
How beautiful the world is in the morning.

Flowers and vegetables, forests tremble.
How beautiful the world is in the morning.
Years ago the garden closed on Adam.
Hold my hand, I hear the waters rising.

COWS

You're always mentioning cows,
how they're sorrowful, or stodgy,
or simply ruminative; how just
because you like milk is not a reason
to meet one, though I wouldn't mind,
particularly on a nice day in a meadow;
and I'd like to meet that author too
whose books I liked, though he is
the one you're really talking about,
not cows at all. When I was 12
I tried to milk a cow, but though
I tugged and tugged no milk
would come: that cow had teats
like rows of rubber gloves, big eyes,
a wicked tail, and I thought of her
when I nursed my first child.
Now here we are in the car driving west
past painted barns and horses
and yes past cows, and our children
have grown beyond milk, and I often
feel like a cow myself, part stodgy,
part sorrowful, and much too ruminative.

Q AND A

I thought I couldn't be surprised:
"Do you write on a computer?" someone
asks, and "Who are your favorite poets?"
and "How much do you revise?"

But when the very young woman
in the fourth row lifted her hand
and without irony inquired:
"Did you write

your Emily Dickinson poem
because you like her work,
or did you know her personally?"
I entered another territory.

"Do I really look that old?"
I wanted to reply, or "Don't
they teach you anything?"
or "What did you just say?"

The laughter that engulfed
the room was partly nervous,
partly simple hilarity.
I won't forget

that little school, tucked
in a lovely pocket of the South,
or that girl whose face
was slowly reddening.

Surprise, like love, can catch
our better selves unawares.
"I've visited her house," I said.
"I may have met her in my dreams."

ON SEEING AN OLD PHOTOGRAPH

Why are the young so beautiful—
a foal or a fledgling sparrow, head
half hidden in a ruff of feathers;
a human infant with that milky,
demanding innocence;
even an adolescent boy, awkwardness
shadowed by grace, in his own
invisible forcefield of desire?

Is it to fool us into sacrifice (remember
Stella Dallas, or a parent bird scouring
the ground for grubs)? To lure the unsuspecting
into the old chain-dance of the genes?
I've looked at you on your way to old age
and found you the perfect portrait
of a man— that wave of white hair
and your noble blade of a nose

like some carved artifact
in a museum. But just now
when I saw the photograph
of you at 20, your feet flung
casually up on your desk, a cigarette—
that ivory amulet, dangling
from supple fingers, and the window
behind you filled to the brim

with leafy spring, I was blindsided
by beauty. I wanted to reach out
and stroke your freshly shaved skin,
to return your sly ambiguous smile,
gateway to some seductive secret.
But out of the frame of the picture,
somewhere beyond that very window,
I was still waiting to be born.

ASH

We fall like leaves,
anonymous as snow,
like ash, like weeds
under some farmer's hoe.

We fear the dark
and watch the light recede.
We know death smiles
on every child conceived.

The moon goes on
relentless in the sky;
in cold complicity
the stars comply.

Remember me.
(How did it grow so late?)
Anonymous,
I turn the page. I wait.

SILENCE

"The language of war is victims."
KHALID SHAIKH MOHAMMED, TERRORIST,
NEW YORK TIMES

If the language of war
is victims,
choose silence.

If its verbs are bullets
seeking their place
in a sentence,

choose silence.
Over the ruined markets
and smoldering streets

the grammar of pain
has exploded
on every tongue;

not even the vowels
of grief are left
to tarnish the air.

The angel of silence
has flown overhead.
Death too is silent.

IN THE FOREST

The trees are lit
from within like Sabbath candles
before they are snuffed out.
Autumn is such a Jewish season,
the whole minor key of it.
Hear how the wind trembles
through the branches, vibrato
as notes of cello music.
Notice the tarnished coppers
and browns, the piles of leaves
just waiting for burning.
Though birds are no longer
in hiding, though children in bright
scarves are kicking the leaves,
I smell the smoke
and remember winter.
Praise what is left.

SOMEWHERE IN THE WORLD

Somewhere in the world
something is happening
which will make its slow way here.

A cold front will come to destroy
the camellias, or perhaps it will be
a heat wave to scorch them.

A virus will move without passport
or papers to find me as I shake
a hand or kiss a cheek.

Somewhere a small quarrel
has begun, a few overheated words
ignite a conflagration,

and the smell of smoke
is on its way;
the smell of war.

Wherever I go I knock on wood—
on tabletops or tree trunks.
I rinse my hands over and over again;

I scan the newspapers
and invent alarm codes which are not
my husband's birthdate or my own.

But somewhere something is happening
against which there is no planning, only
those two aging conspirators, Hope and Luck.

ON THE STEPS OF THE JEFFERSON MEMORIAL

We invent our gods
the way the Greeks did,
in our own image—but magnified.
Athena, the very mother of wisdom,
squabbled with Poseidon
like any human sibling
until their furious tempers
made the sea writhe.

Zeus wore a crown
of lightning bolts one minute,
a cloak of feathers the next,
as driven by earthy lust
he prepared to swoop
down on Leda.
Despite their power,
frailty ran through them

like the darker veins
in the marble of these temples
we call monuments.
Looking at Jefferson now,
I think of the language
he left for us to live by.
I think of the slave
in the kitchen downstairs.

THE ORDINARY

It may happen on a day
of ordinary weather—
the usual assembled flowers,
or fallen leaves
disheveling the grass.
You may be feeding the dog,
or sipping a cup of tea,
and then: the telegram;
or the phone call;
or the sharp pain traveling
the length of your
left arm, or his.
And as your life is switched
to a different track
(the landscape
through grimy windows
almost the same though
entirely different) you wonder
why the wind doesn't
rage and blow as it does
so convincingly
in Lear, for instance.
It is pathetic fallacy
you long for—the roses
nothing but their thorns,
the downed leaves
subjects for a body count.
And as you lie in bed
like an effigy of yourself,
it is the ordinary
that comes to save you—
the china teacup waiting
to be washed, the old dogs
whining to go out.

FLIGHT

They have examined
our luggage, made me
remove my shoes
and then my scarf, as if
I might strangle someone
in its silky purple.
But they let my fear
of flight on board,
though its weight
and turbulence might
bring down any plane.
I signed on for this,
I tell myself, as I did
that other June so long ago,
walking down another aisle
with you, and only
a vague idea of love
to keep us aloft.

TRAVELING LIGHT

I'm only leaving you
for a handful of days,
but it feels as though
I'll be gone forever—
the way the door closes

behind me with such solidity,
the way my suitcase
carries everything
I'd need for an eternity
of traveling light.

I've left my hotel number
on your desk, instructions
about the dog
and heating dinner. But
like the weather front

they warn is on its way
with its switchblades
of wind and ice,
our lives have minds
of their own.

From

Insomnia

2015

INSOMNIA: 3 AM

Sleep has stepped out
for a smoke
and may not be back.

The sun is waiting
in the celestial
green room,

practicing
its flamboyant
entrance.

In the hour of the wolf
there is only
the clock

for company,
ticking
through the dark

remorseless
stations
of the night.

CONSIDER THE SPACE BETWEEN STARS

Consider the white space
between words on a page, not just
the margins around them.

Or the space between thoughts:
instants when the mind is inventing
exactly what it thinks

and the mouth waits
to be filled with language.
Consider the space

between lovers after a quarrel,
the white sheet a cold metaphor
between them.

Now picture the brief space
before death enters, hat in hand:
these vanishing years, filled with light.

LATE IN OCTOBER

Late in October, I watch
it all unravel—the whole
autumn leafery
succumbing to rain.
At the moment
of their most intense beauty,
reds and yellows bleed
into each other
like dried paints on a palette—
those ghosts of pictures
never painted.

Perhaps beauty
is the mother of death,
not the other way around.
Perhaps the rain itself
is an answer: knives
of crystal, cleansing
and killing as it falls.
I turn from the window;
winter is coming next.
White will have
its own perfections.

IN THE ORCHARD

Why are these old, gnarled trees
so beautiful, while I am merely
old and gnarled?

If I had leaves, perhaps, or apples . . .
if I had bark instead
of this lined skin,

maybe the wind would wind itself
around my limbs
in its old sinuous dance.

I shall bite into an apple
and swallow the seeds.
I shall come back as a tree.

FIRST SNOW

The clouds dissolve in snow—
a simple act of physics
or the urge to just let go?

On hills, on frozen lakes
all definition fades
before the rush of flakes

until, bereft of light,
the moon gives up
her sovereign claim to white.

THE GARDENER

He's out rescuing his fallen hollies
after the renegade snowstorm,

sawing their wounded limbs off
quite mercilessly (I think of the scene

in *Kings Row*, the young soldier waking
to find his legs gone).

He's tying up young bamboo—
their delicate tresses litter the driveway—

shoveling a door through the snow
to free the imprisoned azaleas.

I half expect him to tend his trees
with aspirin and soup, the gardener

who finds in destruction
the very reason to carry on;

who would look at the ruins
of Eden and tell the hovering angel

to put down his sword,
there was work to be done.

AFTER THE SNOW

I'm inside
a Japanese woodcut,

snow defining
every surface:

shadows
of tree limbs

like pages
of inked calligraphy;

one sparrow,
high on a branch,

brief as
a haiku.

Here
in the Maryland woods, far

from Kyoto
I enter Kyoto.

EDWARD HOPPER, UNTITLED

An empty theatre: seats
shrouded in white
like rows of headstones;
the curtain about to rise
(or has it fallen?)
on a scene
of transcendental
silence.

And the audience?
A solitary figure sheathed
in black, a woman
in a hat perhaps
(more abstract
shape than woman)
sitting alone
in the cavernous dark.

This is quintessential Hopper—
cliché of loneliness
transformed by brushstroke
into something part paint,
part desperation.
"Oil on board," the label says,
as if even a tree
had to be sacrificed.

ADAM AND EVE

Lucas Cranach the Elder, 1526

She seems a mere girl really,
small breasted and slim,
her body luminescent
next to Adam, who scratches
his head in mild perplexity.
So many baubles hang
from the tree
it didn't hurt to pick one.
The snake is a quicksilver curve
on a branch she is almost
young enough to swing from.

The garden bores her anyway—
no weedy chaos among
the flowers and vegetables;
the animals so tame
you can hardly tell the lamb
from the lion, the doe from the stag
whose antlers outline Adam's modesty.
She is like that teen-age girl
who wandered from the mall last week
not to be seen again, the world before her
glittering and perilous.

FIREFLIES

here come
the fireflies

with their staccato
lights

their tiny headlamps
blinking

in silence
through the tall grass

like constellations
cut loose

from the night
sky

(see how desire
transforms

the plainest
of us)

or flashes of insight
that flare

for a moment
then flicker out

IMAGINARY CONVERSATION

You tell me to live each day
as if it were my last. This is in the kitchen
where before coffee I complain
of the day ahead—that obstacle race
of minutes and hours,
grocery stores and doctors.

But why the last? I ask. Why not
live each day as if it were the first—
all raw astonishment, Eve rubbing
her eyes awake that first morning,
the sun coming up
like an ingénue in the East?

You grind the coffee
with the small roar of a mind
trying to clear itself. I set
the table, glance out the window
where dew has baptized every
living surface.

IN THE HAPPO-EN GARDEN, TOKYO

The way a birthmark
on a woman's face defines
rather than mars
her beauty,

so the skyscrapers—
those flowers of technology—
reveal the perfection
of the garden they surround.

Perhaps Eden is buried
here in Japan,
where an incandescent
koi slithers snakelike

to the edge of the pond;
where a black-haired
Eve-san in the petaled
folds of a kimono

once showed her silken body
to the sun, then picked a persimmon
and with a small bow
bit into it.

RIVER PIG

"So you like fugu," his Japanese host remarked
after my husband unwittingly ate the sushi
which can kill if not cleaned properly. River pig
it's also called. I'm glad I wasn't there.
But I remember a dinner where I preemptively
told my mushroom-gathering host
I was allergic to mushrooms. When he served
the cultivated kind I love, I had to refuse them.

And I remember puffer fish we caught and ate at the beach—
those distant relatives to fugu, though I didn't know it then.
The mushrooms that grow in our woods now
are every shape and size: the honey fungus and the hen of the woods,
the smoky bracket. Some are as short and tough
as bruised thumbs, some like tiny fringed umbrellas.
They cling to trees or bivouac their armies on the grass.
Often they sprout like bad thoughts, overnight.

But under a canopy of fallen leaves, the delicate
chanterelles also hide, which people fry
in sizzling butter and devour. I never dared.
How well the dangerous can camouflage itself—
the temper that flares like lightning
from a sunny disposition; the switchblade
hiding in a well-tailored pocket.
Some women like a hint of danger in their men,

as sexy as the edge the thought of crashing
gives skydivers. I've always chosen safety.
But I'm haunted now (too late) by what I've missed:
that trip down a green and sinuous river. The man I said no to.
I don't eat raw fish. I choose the most benign (entombed
in plastic) mushrooms. As if I want to arrive at death
quite safe from harm, and innocent, locking the coffin lid
behind me so nothing dangerous can get in.

SHIP'S CLOCK

The ship's clock, stowed in a box
for its passage to the beach each summer,
continues to chime every 4 hours
(first watch . . . dog watch . . .)
inside the cedar closet.

I look up from my desk and wonder
what that rounded sound could be,
then remember the clock,
all polished brass, still marking
the watches of a distant ocean.

So a prisoner might sing,
alone in a cell; or the songbird
serenade bright fronds
of leaf and fern, though caged
in the dark of a northern city.

The bird has its arias,
the clock its mathematics.
I string words together
wherever I am—
in planes, in waiting rooms,

forcing the actual to sink
and disappear
beneath the bright
and shimmering surface
of the half imagined.

AT MAHO BAY: FOR JON

The pelicans are putting on a show—
breakfast for them means some poor fish must die.
We search the wreaths of coral far below

where golden hamlets flutter, blueheads glow,
all of it sweetest nectar for the eye,
while pelicans are putting on their show.

Is it amnesia these brief days bestow
on you and me whose lives are speeding by?
We search the reefs of coral far below

forgetting for the moment what we know
of illness, wintry weeping, of goodbye.
The pelicans are putting on a show.

The sand between our fingers seems to flow
as through an hourglass: time can only fly.
We search the wreaths of coral far below.

A plane is waiting, is it time to go?
Was so much turquoise beauty just a lie?
The pelicans are putting on a show.
We searched the wreaths of coral far below.

AH, FRIEND

in the black hood,
come! Pierce
my heart

with the sharp ring
of the doorbell;
throw pebbles

at my window
with the perilous sound
of hail on a tin roof.

No more of these
odd hints: a feather
of blood here,

a shadow, the size
of a thumbprint,
on an X-ray there.

I will never be more ready
than I am now,
as I sit

peeling a tangerine
and turning the brittle pages
in the long book

of my life. I won't
even need to pack
for the journey.

LAST RITES

She's given up sex.
She's given up travel.
She's given up the rush
of alcohol to the brain
at the first sip of wine—
that sweet burn
as it slips down the throat.
And her quarrels,
her celebrations,
she's given them up too
as she's given up books—
their pages too heavy to turn.
What's left is a blur
of sky where the weather
rehearses its own finales.
What's left is blue emptiness
behind the white sail
of the nurse's starched cap,
steering her out to sea.

MUSINGS BEFORE SLEEP

The lines on my face are starting
to make me look like photographs
of Auden in old age. If the lines
of my poems could also be
as incandescent as his,
would I be willing to look
as worn and wrinkled?
I avoid mirrors now,
particularly when the strong light
of morning reveals what I don't wish to see,
and sometimes I want to erase
the words I'm putting down,
even as my pen touches
the paper. Sometimes I feel guilty
about growing old and forgetful
and sometimes guilty about spending
so much time tinkering with language,
though tinkering isn't the word
most writers would use—revision,
we say, which is sometimes holy,
and also something many women do:
revise their faces with rouge or stitches.
Are there two kinds of vanity—
vanity about the beauty
we are born with or without,
and vanity about the beauty
we try to make out of the sticks
and stones of language?
Old age should be a time
of accepting the hand dealt out,
in fact already almost played out.

But in these moments when sleep
is about to take me, when I might be
any age at all, I think again of Auden who,
for the length of a dream at least,
may hold my all too human head
in the hands that wrote those poems.

From

A Dog Runs

Through It

2018

THE GREAT DOG OF NIGHT

John Wilde, oil on panel

The great dog of night
growls at the windows,
barks at the door.

Soon I must straddle
its sleek back and fly
over the fields

and rooftops
of sleep, above us
a vague moon

loose in the sky,
far ahead of us
morning.

THE NEW DOG

Into the gravity of my life,
the serious ceremonies
of polish and paper and pen, has come

this manic animal
whose innocent disruptions
make nonsense
of my old simplicities.

As if I needed him
to prove again that after
all the careful planning
anything can happen.

DOMESTIC ANIMALS

The animals in this house
have dream claws and teeth
and shadow the rooms
at night, their furled tails dangerous.
In the morning, all sweet slobber,
the dog may yawn, the cat
make cat sounds deep
in its furred throat.
And who would guess
how they wait for dark
when into the green
jungle of our sleep
they insinuate
themselves, releasing
their terrible hunger.

IN THE WALLED GARDEN

In the walled garden
where my illusions grow,
the lilac, watered, blooms all winter,
and innocence grows like moss
on the north side of every tree.
No ax or mower resides here—
green multiplies unimpeded—
and every morning all the dogs
of my long life jump up
to lick my face.
My father rests behind a hedge,
bard of my storied childhood,
and in the fading half-life of ambition,
wanting and having merge.
Here flowers and flesh don't wither.
Here you will never leave me.
Here poetry will save the world.

I AM LEARNING TO ABANDON THE WORLD: FOR M

I am learning to abandon the world
before it can abandon me.
Already I have given up the moon
and snow, closing my shades
against the claims of white.
And the world has taken
my father, my friend.
I have given up melodic lines of hills,
moving to a flat, tuneless landscape.
And every night I give my body up
limb by limb, working upwards
across bone, towards the heart.
But morning comes with small
reprieves of coffee and birdsong.
A tree outside the window
which was simply shadow moments ago
takes back its branches twig
by leafy twig.
And as I take my body back
the sun lays its warm muzzle on my lap
as if to make amends.

The sun is up,
the sun is always up.
The silent "e"
keeps watch,
and 26 strong stones
can build a wall of syllables
for Nell and Ned
and Ann.

Rab was such a good dog,
Mother. We left him
under the big tree
by the brook
to take care of the dolls
and the basket.

But Rab has run away.
The basket's gone back to reeds
through which the night wind
blows; and mother was erased;
the dolls are painted harlots
in the Doll's Museum.

Where did it go, Rose?
I don't know;
away off, somewhere.
The fat hen
has left the nest.

I hand my daughter
this dusty book.
Framed in her window
the sky darkens to slate,
a lexicon of wandering stars.

Listen, child—the barking
in the distance
is Rab the dog star
trotting home
for dinner.

PLUTO

There's the planet, of course,
with its icy outcroppings, its moons,

and plutonium, which will light our way
to the future, if it doesn't destroy us.

And plutocrat means wealth,
from the Greek, or power.

But for me it's the dog
with the shiny nose and the standup ears

who clowned his way through
my sober childhood.

ARGOS

Shaggy and incontinent,
I have become the very legend
of fidelity. I am
more famous than the dog star
or those hounds of Charon's
who nip at a man's ankles
on his way to the underworld.
Even Penelope wanted
proof, and Eurykleia
had to see a scar.
But I knew what I knew—
what else are noses for?
Men are such needy creatures,
Zeus himself comes to them
as an animal. I'll take
my place gladly
among the bones and fleas
of this fragrant dung heap
and doze my doggy way
through history.

THE ANIMALS

When I see a suckling pig turn
on the spit, its mouth around
an apple, or feel the soft
muzzle of a horse
eating a windfall from my hand,
I think about the animals
when Eden closed down,
who stole no fruit themselves.

After feeding so long
from Adam's outstretched hand
and sleeping under the mild stars,
flank to flank,
what did they do on freezing nights?
Still ignorant of nests and lairs
did they try to warm themselves
at the fiery leaves of the first autumn?

And how did they learn to sharpen
fangs and claws? Who taught them
the first lesson: that flesh
had been transformed to meat?
Tiger and Bear, Elk and Dove.
God saved them places on the Ark,
and Christ would honor them with
parables, calling himself the Lamb of God.

We train our dogs in strict obedience
at which we failed ourselves.
But sometimes the sound of barking
fills the night like distant artillery,
a sound as chilling as the bellow
of steers led up the ramps
of cattle cars whose gates swing
shut on them, as Eden's did.

OLD JOKE

The children all are grown, the dog has died;
the old joke says that now life can begin,
the creaking door to freedom open wide.
But old age seems my fault, a kind of sin
precluding guilty pleasures—food and drink
the luxuries of travel, even books.

Depression is the bed in which I sink,
my body primed for pain's insidious hooks:
the swollen fingers and the stiffened back;
the way regret can pierce you with its knife;
the migraines like some medieval rack;
the winnowing of loved ones from my life.

For months I carried that old dog around
helping her eat and cleaning up her mess.
Though she was deaf, I talked to her—each sound
the rough equivalent of a caress.
If memories are like the poems I wrote
but didn't think quite good enough to save,

and if the final wisdoms I would quote
await that cold anthology: the grave,
then let the sun, at least, become a shawl
keeping me wrapped in warmth until the end;
my lawn a place where children's children sprawl
next to the shy ghost of my canine friend.

ENVOI

We're signing up for heartbreak,
We know one day we'll rue it.
But oh the way our life lights up
The years a dog runs through it.